67 Years

Erin Lovelien

67 Years

A Story of Life, Love, & Small-Town America

Erin Lovelien

Fishtail Publishing

Published in the USA by Fishtail Publishing, LLC
Reynoldsburg, Ohio

Contact Information
Email: fishtailpublishing@gmail.com
Website: fishtailpublishing.org

Dedicated to my loving grandparents, and the legacy of love they gifted to us all.

Keep Smiling.

This work was originally performed as a 60-minute fringe during the 2022 Northlands Storytelling Network Fringe Festival.

In this journey through life and love, Erin travels to the small town in Pennsylvania where her maternal grandparents met and began their legacy. As she takes a stroll through history, she wonders how such profound compassion and service became the foundation of the Yarletts name. How is it that some can love so deeply, while others are left pining for connection? In the months after her grandparents' 67th wedding anniversary, Erin reflects on her own adventures in searching for love and living with a heart wide open.

After years of dreaming what her future might look like, and months of meticulous planning, the day had finally arrived. She could hear them clearly: wedding bells.

It was an embracing fall day, the trees wrapped in coordinated colors of their own. Family and friends traveled from near and far to celebrate and bear witness to a love that was only just beginning; a story that was just writing its first chapters.

Her heartbeat shook the fingers that were wrapped tightly around her bouquet, but her feet stood firmly at the threshold of the aisle entrance. With a momentary pause, though void of doubt, she nodded with a quiet anticipation, and the towering doors were opened. As she took her first steps into a room filled with admiring eyes, all she could see was him.

Tradition wrapped its blessings around them as they spoke their vows and promised one another in good times and in bad, in sickness and in health. And as the rings were exchanged, she shifted nervously with anticipation of what was yet to come. They smiled at one another, and as the officiant announced their legal union, their wedded names spoken aloud for the very first time, she closed her eyes. She leaned in. For a moment, all was still.

But, then she felt him…squeeze her hand. Her eyes snapped open and she looked up to find him grinning. Before she knew it she was flying down the aisle, pulled in one direction by her sister who was trying to hand off her bouquet, and in the other by her now-husband who was speeding toward the door.

As they spilled out onto the steps of the church, the ceremony falling into a blur behind them, he turned to her and said with a mischievous smile, "Your mother asked me not to kiss you in front of the congregation." Then, he held her tightly, knowing the rest of his life would change with this very moment, and for the first time, they kissed as husband and wife.

In that moment, kissing on the steps outside of the church, my maternal grandparents had no way of knowing how their union would impact generations to come.

.−.. . −−. . −−.−. −.−−

I have always been enamored by my grandparents' relationship. There is something about its simplicity that makes it seemingly intangible and unrealistic. What makes their love truly astounding is how it fills their own cups and then spills over into the world that surrounds them.

When Carol's family moved to Pennsylvania, back when she was just learning to walk, they did not move to any address in particular. Down in the valley of rolling hillsides, a handful of houses dotted a quiet main road that ran perpendicular to the Shenango River. From that river's edge to the end of the neighborhood, marked by the Volunteer Fire Department, it was just over a quarter mile's walk. The post office was to Pulaski what a local bar would be in neighboring cities; a stop on the way home where you would find your buddies kicking back with a beer and a glowing cigarette. In this small-town America, kids played freely in the streets until someone standing on a nearby porch herded them home for dinner; neighbors baked each other pies for no reason. Amish horses and buggies plodded through town, clip-clopping their way to the mill and back. You could leave the small town of Pulaski just as quickly and unceremoniously as you entered it.

Just on the edge of town, on the corner of routes 208 and 551—which were not, in fact, 208 and 551 at the time—was a big white house where Carol and her family lived. And just a stone's throw away from that house on the corner, down a quiet side street branching off from the main road, was where her next story would begin.

When Carol Joan Cox and Charles Lester Yarletts fell in love, Pulaski had not yet been assigned a zip code.

Carol's father was an intelligent Navy man, while her mother was a strong-willed homemaker. Although outward displays of affection were not necessarily a primary love language in her household growing up, the importance of kindness and community never went unnoticed in Carol's young life. Her father devoted his knowledge to establishing electrical engineering classes in high schools along the coast of New Jersey and all the way to Atlantic City. He was a reliably calm, composed, and optimistic man. Although he might not have said those three profound words very often, Carol's father is remembered for being someone who lived his life in a way that spoke love into the world around him.

While Carol found her love of learning and quick intellect from her father, her mother inspired within her a determined self-sufficiency and deep care for others. Raising six kids on her own while her husband served his eight years in the navy, Carol's mother continued to be a scout leader, volunteer at church, and give selflessly to those in need. She gave herself to her children and yet still found space for her neighbors. But, despite being an attentive and devoted mother, she longed for a husband who was more present and a place where she could truly call home. She was a Pennsylvania woman at heart, living in an unfamiliar and isolated place on the nation's coast. The family's move to Pulaski several years later was driven by her deep desire to belong.

At twelve years old, Charles—or, more affectionately known as Charlie—had a rambunctious spirit that could hardly be contained within the sprawling fields of Amish country. In fact, he worked quite hard to avoid sitting still by helping out on his grandfather's farm, playing basketball with his buddies in New Bedford, or even cleaning the Presbyterian church after school. In those days, it didn't matter that he was Methodist and spent his Sundays in the chapel down the block.

Charlie loved being on his grandfather's dairy farm. Although he wasn't so much a fan of bailing hay or cleaning the stables, he thrived on fresh air and open spaces. And, still to this day, you can't get through a family meal without Charlie asking for a nice tall glass of buttermilk.

A young boy true to the times, he sometimes found peculiar ways to amuse himself on long afternoons in the countryside. One of his more "helpful" activities was to collect stones from the property, line up the rocks along the edge of the harvesting fields, and chuck them one by one at the birds trying to snack on the produce. A champion of peaches and protector of tomatoes, Charlie used his improving aim to ensure his grandfather's livelihood. However, with time and a bit of competitive spirit, Charlie began to wonder how he could better track his accuracy and continue to strengthen his throwing arm.

So, he took to throwing the apples that had fallen off of the trees. With a piece of chalk he had pocketed earlier that day from the blackboard at school, he drew a large circle and then a smaller circle on the side of a weathered barn. He picked up the fruit and paced backward to the line of pine trees that bordered the farm property: *ka-thunk, ka-thunk, ka-thunk.*

After several weeks of this, Charlie's grandfather complained to his father, "Your son is making a mess of my barnyard, George. Every night, when I bring in the cows, they wander off to eat the fruit instead. Tell that boy to find another activity."

Now, looking for a new challenge, Charlie was wandering through the pastures when he came across a hen laying eggs in the tall grass. Charlie bent down on all fours and combed through the grasses where he found several more hidden eggs. As he walked back to the coop, he realized that eggs not laid inside it would never really be missing. So, one by one, he lifted an egg into his palm and aimed for a small discolored section of the weathered barn. Before it could leave his hand, the shell shattered, and Charlie looked down to find his arm dripping in yolk. Pleased with his efforts and up for the challenge, he continued collecting eggs in the field and refining the art of the perfect pitch.

Weeks went by before his grandfather came upon the sticky mess of eggshells behind the chicken coop. Once again, he approached his son and said, "George, you've got to have a talk with that boy of yours. He's making a mess of my chicken coop."

Later that week, Charlie was finishing his supper when his father walked into the kitchen, set a gift on the table, and quietly walked away. Charlie put his fork down and, watching his father retreat back to the living room, carefully picked up from the table a brand new baseball glove. It would be another 60 years until that very glove would retire.

Just like his baseball glove, it seemed as though things back then were made to last. So, as I reflected on their 67 long years of marriage, I began to wonder what it was about my grandparents' love story that just doesn't seem replicable now. Why does it often feel as though a love like theirs is far from reach? Was there something in the air in Pulaski, Pennsylvania, or has small-town America become so obsolete that the values once ingrained in families across the nation are now simply less accessible? Have we been so focused on obtaining more of the world, that we've forgotten to appreciate what was next door the whole time?

Anyone you ask today would tell you that my grandpa Charlie would give the shirt off his back to anyone in need. That is, assuming he was wearing one at the time. My grandmother, Carol, meanwhile, would be the first to spend hours in the kitchen preparing a meal for anyone experiencing hardship. Coming together as a community and supporting one another through challenging times wasn't just a nice way to live in the 1950s; it was the only way of life they knew.

During a particularly terrible snowstorm in high school, Charlie and Carol took a sled through town, collecting eggs and milk from the local farms and making deliveries to doorsteps, so that those who couldn't travel by foot wouldn't go hungry.

Sportsmanship was at the core of everything Charlie did. Even when his football coaches told him to, "Hit 'em hard," and, "Knock 'em out of the game," he never did. He played to win, but he would never be the reason that another player would be out for the season. To this day, he approaches conflict the same way. "People are like that," he'll say. "You can tell them they're wrong or that they're being mean, but you never punch back."

In my grandmother's diary from 1952, she documented the many bake sales, scouts meetings, neighborhood-wide turkey roasts, and last-minute calls to babysit when someone in town needed help.

You simply can't read about Pulaski, PA in those times without the impression that community was the foundation of all life.

In his later years, Charlie started up a basketball camp for kids with the hope that teaching them the value of hard work and practice would help prepare them for discipline in the classroom. He wanted to instill in them the value of camaraderie on the court that would lead to a life focused on community. He coached kids on Saturday morning from all over the region, free of charge. He even bought tennis shoes and socks with his own wallet for any child that needed gear to play.

And, in the months leading up to his 90th birthday in 2022, Charlie confessed, "Every night I have a list of 42 people that I pray for. I name them one by one, and ask God to take care of them. But, sometimes, I wonder who is taking care of God while he's busy taking care of everyone else." Charles Lester Yarletts is the only man I know who prays **for** God.

--- .-. .. --. .. -. ...

I wanted to understand what made my grandparents, and their love, so profound. Is it a product of their faith? The influence of their parents? Is it because small-town America in the 1950s was such a drastically different landscape to today's Internet-hungry world? Is it because of their hardships, or because of their resilience?

Like any kid experiencing magic for the first time, I wanted to know how the trick was done. So, I decided to walk their origin story, to feel the embrace of a quaint town, stand on the steps of their church, and exist beneath the lingering glow of their five-cell flashlights as they discovered a sort of love that seems to only exist in fairy tales.

On a particularly cold and snow-covered February weekend, I headed to Pennsylvania to find out how small-town hearts were made.

I sat in a local establishment that was still run by its original owner, where pictures of the 1981 Wilmington High baseball team's championship win still hung on the wall. From the corner booth in Ryder's Restaurant I could hear the clip-clopping and clattering of an Amish buggy sailing through the four-way intersection out front. It was a brisk day in New Wilmington, and as the winter sky became hazed with snow, I chewed my All-American bacon cheeseburger and watched the 18th century appear to bind seamlessly with the modern world.

From across the booth, my mom rattled off dates, names, and buildings that may or may not still exist. I would soon find myself transported by the stories emblazoned into the memories of generations. But, as powerful as I know a story can be, I still felt the persistent longing to understand its origins.

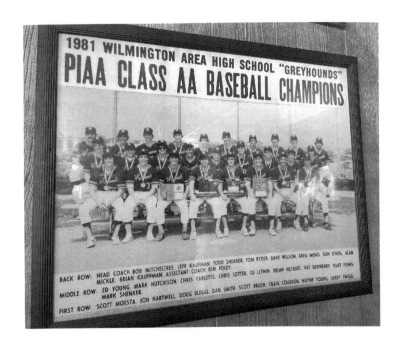

Despite my grandparents being three years apart, they studied in the same classroom due to Charlie's humble beginnings in an Amish schoolhouse, one of few academic options available at the time. Within the sturdy walls of a brick elementary school, Charlie and Carol's lifelong friendship and love story began.

From a stack of class materials, a teacher would pull out an attendance register and open it wide across her desk. As the teacher called roll, Carol would sit and picture the house of each student. She knew that William lived in the duplex next to Mr. McMahon's Car Repair. She could picture Doris's family piling into their dark green station wagon outside their two-story home near the square. Timothy lived just outside of the town limits in a small farmhouse with particularly noisy chickens, and Sally walked to school everyday from the apple orchard that would soon become famous for its spiced donuts. Then, there was Charlie, a handsome but rambunctious character she had known since she was a toddler, when their families lived side-by-side in a humble duplex in New Bedford.

Although Charlie always recognized the importance of a good education, as he would later encourage his kids and grandkids to work hard and stay in school, academics was never Charlie's personal strong suit. He enjoyed history class and even dabbled in Shakespeare's iambic pentameter, but he'd much rather have been in the expansive fields of his grandfather's farm, or stepping up to the pitcher's mound to take on the Plain Grove boys.

Carol, on the other hand, was an avid academic study and natural-born teacher. One day, she offered to help Charlie with his homework on the bus ride home. This quickly became their routine until they graduated together several years later from Union High School.

Long into their newfound friendship, well after the games had been won, the chores were done, and choir practices were over, Charlie and Carol would grab their five-cell flashlights and head to a bedroom window. With the upper level of their homes at just the right angle to see down the block, they would greet each other: .. -- / .... --- -- . "I'm home." What they learned in scouts they put to good use, flirting by way of a single bulb, pulsing through the night. Morse code was, perhaps, their first love language.

I hugged my coat tighter around my neck as I crawled out of the front seat of the car. Baseball season in Pulaski was still several months away, and the snow-covered ground in the park crunched beneath my boots. I thrust my heels into the Earth to prevent slipping and clamored my way up to the tall chain-link fence, where a large green sign hung haphazardly from behind home plate: *Adam Grell Field, Lawrence County Historical Society, Sports Hall of Honor.* This field was a sacred place for America's favorite pastime and where two very different love stories unfolded simultaneously.

After two decades of the same affectionate recitations, I could envision the stories I had heard growing up; my grandpa stepping up to the mound, his glove tucked behind his right thigh.

I stood against the fence, the snow seeming to melt before my eyes to reveal a freshly groomed infield and bleachers of spectators. As I closed my eyes, I could practically feel the mid-summer, afternoon sun warming my shoulders. I took in the energized summer breeze as dust enveloped the players in the infield. And then, there he was, the stories and characters coming to life in real time. I could see a young Charlie as he glanced over to third base, and then methodically over to first. Beads of sweat fell from his forehead, congealing on the dusty ground beneath him. I held my breath as he nodded at the catcher and lifted his chest.

Just as he reached for the baseball in his glove, I could hear the faint creaking of a distant screen door. From his peripheral, and from my vantage point behind home plate, we both watched as a familiar figure emerged from the house across the street. A youthful Carol made her way onto the back porch of the big white house on the corner, where she leaned into the sun and waved her dishtowel in the air.

I smiled as Charlie reached up to remove his baseball cap. He wiped the sweat from his forehead with intention and, still gripping the rim of his cap, seemed to nod to no one in particular; their unspoken hello. Grandma clutched her dish towel and I let out a gentle sigh, knowing that even in the most critical of moments on the field, Charlie was always thinking about her. From her porch, Carol watched as Charlie leaned back and launched a curveball straight into the catcher's mitt. The final strike.

Baseball wasn't just America's favorite pastime of the decade, it was the blood that ran through Charlie's veins. But baseball wasn't the only thing that kept Charlie's heart beating.

My grandparents were married in the Pulaski Methodist Church on September 11th, 1954. Not wanting to appear exclusive, they issued invitations by word of mouth only. Although they expected the church to be filled with friends and family coming from near and far, just moments before the ceremony began there was a frantic search for extra chairs. The pews were packed and the back was becoming standing room only. The building pulsed with enthusiasm as Carol walked down the aisle toward the man with whom she would create a long-lasting legacy of love.

After a celebratory reception in the Presbyterian church across the street, they took a honeymoon to Niagara Falls and returned to Pulaski where they rented a house that sat equidistant to each of their childhood homes. They both wanted a family, but they both wanted to give their children the greatest opportunities for academic success and personal development. So, they later relocated to New Wilmington, a bustling college town just 10 minutes due East, where Charlie drove a truck and Carol worked for Ryber Cadillac. By the time she graduated from Westminster College, they were happily expecting the birth of Charles Jr., my Uncle Chuckie.

Motherhood, I've been told, is an enduring and unfathomably exhausting terrain. Yet, my grandma Carol remained steadfastly certain that she was destined for parenthood, and not just any parenthood, at that.

As I stood on the corner of New Castle and Vine Street, I noticed the wind carried with it the faint voices of children from a schoolyard that once was. With the stained yellow brick of my mother's childhood house behind me, I followed

the voices and the patter of small feet as they trekked their half-block journey to the elementary school.

My grandmother was surrounded by young hearts in those days, but that didn't keep her from pining for more of her own.

With Chuckie and the light he brought into their world, my grandparents yearned for another. Carol Lynne was joyfully welcomed into their arms a short 13 months after Chuckie was born. With her little ones still little, Carol followed her passion and became a school teacher, spending long days substituting in one-room Amish schoolhouses and eventually having her own classroom at the elementary school on West Vine Street. Despite her blooming career and passion for awakening the minds of the town's youngest, she and her husband longed for a third child to complete their home.

It was during her early years of teaching that my grandmother began to experience the distressing pattern of the joy of hope met with the heartbreak of loss. They kept trying, and yet they kept feeling the full weight of involuntary absence. She felt time after time after time the betrayal of her own womb.

Decades later, on a hot afternoon in Florida, I sat at the kitchen table with my heart in my throat. "Grandma, how many babies did you…" I couldn't bear the weight of the full question, but she heard what hung in the air between us. She set her dishtowel on the counter, her chin tilted in thought, "Fourteen, I think." She casually turned back to the sink and began scrubbing a pan.

I could no longer see the pain of loss in her eyes, yet I had to imagine the breadth of its power still remained. I was staring down at my plate when she added, "You know, I carried a few to full term." She remained focused on the dishwater, "Once, I was out on the playground with the kids. Those were the days that physical activity was mandated in the classroom. We were doing our exercises together and I felt something…change. I wrote the headteacher a note and walked home. I gave birth that day, but he was already gone."

She went on to tell me about a particularly rare and upsetting pregnancy, one that left doctors in awe and her with a higher risk of developing cancer. But once she was medically cleared and ready to try again, try they did. And, suddenly, a woman I had long admired for her independence and compassion transformed before my eyes into a true immortal force of love. I couldn't fathom experiencing so much heartbreak and still remaining strong enough to keep going.

I couldn't help but ask, "Grandma, if you don't mind me asking…why did you keep trying?" She shrugged, "I wanted three kids, and the doctors didn't tell me to stop. That wasn't something they did often in those days."

She spoke of her determination as though it were a recipe for baking pie. I took a drink of water to keep my jaw from sinking to the floor. Six long years after my mom was born, they brought their third and final pride and joy, Christopher, into the world.

Their **love** story was simple. But their love **story** was not. It was written with magic but consumed by reality. There was joy, but there was also significant loss. Yet, through it all, they remained steadfastly confident that love and kindness and family are what matters most in this world. Rather than build an empire of wealth, they built a kingdom of selfless and compassionate human beings. And that was the answer to a rich life.

In each of my grandparents' three children exists the truest form of love. They were brought into this world with persistent longing and unconditional adoration. They were destined to fill the world with as much love and grace as it took to bring them into it.

I was quickly learning that while love stories themselves can be complicated, love itself is a simple choice. If there's anything that my grandparents' love story has taught me, it's that love is a practice; it's an energy you put out into the world with your whole self, a gift that expects nothing in return, a glue that holds two equally enamored individuals together. Love is supportive, curious, and kind. Love is 67 years, despite the losses and hardship. It is 67 years of a beautiful thing.

I always longed for a love like Carol and Charlie's. I longed for a partner I could grow old with, who would still hold my hand in the grocery store at 85 years old, and who would tell anyone and everyone how proud they are to be mine. I yearned for someone to kiss me on the steps, knowing that his life would forever be changed.

But, I'm a suburban girl at heart. I grew up in a quiet neighborhood surrounded by noisy city life in Columbus, Ohio. Small-town America was something that only existed in the generations of stories I heard growing up. I slowly began to wonder if a love like my grandparents' would ever be possible in the world in which I lived.

I grew up on a diet of Disney princesses and Hallmark movies. To me, true love was achievable with the right combination of looking irresistibly disheveled and accidentally stumbling into the right wrong classroom. Did I spend years walking into the wrong classroom with the hope of locking eyes with a stranger? I'll never tell. But I will tell you that the daydream of finding my prince charming in some questionable and undeniably cheesy way was never far from reach.

There was Collin, who I met while pretending to be a lawyer during a summer camp program called, *You're On Trial*. The Legally Blonde energy was a little too real and when he started writing me warm fuzzies, the rest was history. At least, for that one short week on campus.

Then there was Chase, who I fell madly in love with while he dramatically read the ingredients from the back of a can of Minute Maid® Lemonade. He was surrounded by swooning middle school girls, yet, I was the one he asked to the dance. He moonwalked his way into my life and I was convinced he was the one. That is, until he left me for his co-star in *The Music Man*. There was trouble in River City, all right.

Then, there was Alex, who bought me pearl earrings and invited me to fly on his family's private jet. As long as I pretended to enjoy fishing and regularly rinsed and repeated the sentence, "For the love of God, Alex, put down the video game controller and do your homework."

At this young point in my life, my relationships seemed short-lived and surface-level. But, I assumed that's what love might be; holding hands through a movie neither one of you really want to watch until you finally leave the theatre and drive through a Wendy's so you can pretend like you're happy to share your Frosty and fries. Love is, compromise?

It wasn't all flirtatious laughter and salty smiles, though. No, my fairy godmother was a little late to the show on a few of the men I dated. One of them took me on a date to Five Guys. Which, let me just add, was embarrassing enough because my definition of an undeniably good burger in those days was a single burger patty on a bun, dipped in ketchup. Yes, dipped in ketchup; I achieve the perfect ketchup-to-burger ratio with every bite.

Not only did I end up getting laughed out of Five Guys on our first date, but my first date also decides that his definition of an undeniably good burger is one that involves mustard, pickles, and massive heaps of onions. When I tell you that our faces became repelling magnets when he leaned in for a kiss later that evening, I mean, it was...awkward. The fumes seeping from that man's mouth were undoubtably vomit-inducing. We did the midwestern goodbye dance for what felt like a whole other date until the poor guy finally got the hint and headed for the door.

Then, there was Twix boy, who took me to see a movie about the anti-bullying movement and then refused to take me home until I agreed to be his girlfriend. And, that's all I have to say about that one.

My final flop sent me head over heels for an over-excited wantrepreneur with anger management issues who tried to convince me that downing Adderall would change my life for the better. When he ditched me on my birthday and moved to the Dominican Republic, I thought, "You know what? They can keep him."

It wasn't long after he left that I decided to forget the whole thing. I spent so many years looking for my other half; the man that would finally complete me. The man who would rescue me from my musings and help me see the light. I began to think that maybe this fairytale thing was overrated.

My grandparents got really lucky - they grew up in a small town. We just don't live in a world like that anymore. No, we live in a strange world of Tinder, Bumble, and Blueberry, or whatever the kids are using these days. An endless binge of scrolling past potentials, day-dreaming that the heart you seek is one swipe away.

Well, I decided that I was done waiting. I decided I didn't need a prince after all. I was a strong, fiercely independent, and intelligent woman with a sense of adventure. I didn't need a man for that.

Even after I met my soul mate at a small New Year's Eve gathering, I kept my eyes on the prize. When I received an offer to move across the globe for six months after graduation, I didn't stop to think about what it might mean for us. I knew he would leave. *Who wouldn't?* But, when I told him my plans, and that I understood if this ended our journey together, he said, plain as day, "I've waited my whole life for you. What's six months more?"

When Josh proposed to me on the back patio of our new home four and a half years later, "Yes" just didn't seem powerful enough.

Though I never doubted the strength of my grandparents' love for one another, the truest depth of their commitment became clear to me just over a year ago. It was an April Fools' Day like most others; I spent the morning avoiding the persistent "comics" in my life and any suspicious chairs with unusually bulky cushions. I then spent the early afternoon packing for our trip to Florida. It was going to be a long drive, but one that would delightfully result in a week and a half with Charlie and Carol, and some of my favorite people on the planet.

My mom, now fiancé, Josh, and I piled our bags in the car, checked the locks on the front door, and began our usual game of, "I feel like I'm forgetting something."

That was when my mom got a little more quiet than usual.

She paused and said, "I need to give you a bit of an update." When my mom says this, no matter the tone, things are probably not about to go your way. Whether it's a simple change in schedule that means you need to shift your plans around a bit, or something more challenging has happened, it's often a similar tone. It's the familiar tune we all learned to sing in preparation for the difficult news to follow. I often attribute this to her long background in healthcare and working in environments in which bad news should always be delivered with a bit of emotional distance and a certain err of professionalism.

"What's going on, Mom?" I felt my heart thumping against the cage of my chest. Josh reached over and took my hand, as though he already knew what was yet to be said.

"He had another TIA."

It felt like the ground sunk a foot deeper into the Earth. My grandpa Charlie had experienced a series of transient ischemic attacks over the past few years but, fortunately—although incredibly scary for us all—none of them were life-threatening. He always recovered well and continued to enthusiastically partake in his favorite pastime of driving my grandma crazy. But this time, I could tell, was different.

I was wracking my brain for something to say, but all I could think was, "APRIL FOOLS!" My mom hugged me tightly and it was then that I could feel her wanting to collapse into my arms. Over her lifetime of nursing and her young career working in HIV/AIDS—where she held the hands of dying patients whose families had disowned them—she built herself as a pillar of resilience and force of love. She is always someone I can count on to be strong for my brother and me, she is a constant course of strength for her patients, coworkers, and friends. But sometimes, love overpowers poise, and the dam just can't withstand the pressure. It would take several days and many more sleepless nights for that pressure to finally find its release. I felt the space around me shift as a layer of armor wrapped itself around my own outer shell. I, too, would be strong because I had to.

As we pulled onto the highway to head south, my grandfather was being admitted to the ER by way of ambulance. The 18-hour journey simultaneously dragged on forever and barely lasted a moment. As we three shared the burden of driving, I took refuge in the backseat as my only space to try and process, undetected under a blanket of midnight on an empty freeway. I knew the day would eventually come that goodbyes would be said, but it could not possibly be now. My brain was flooded with what-ifs and why now's, knowing that even an answer couldn't possibly calm my anxious heart.

We drove straight to the hospital. By the time we arrived, I had been awake for 23 hours straight. Josh and I sat in the parking lot while my mom went inside to try and talk to the nurses. I felt the heartbreak of so many families left standing on the outside of windows, as COVID-19 left their loved ones inside to cope alone. I sat in the driver's seat while Josh slept in the back, my eyes burning and my body restless, but sleep far from possible.

My great Aunt and her fiancé picked us up and drove us to the house where my grandma was pacing in the kitchen. My grandfather's absence, even for just one night, was devastatingly unfamiliar. After I showered off the last 24 hours and tried hopelessly to revive my exhausted eyes, I emerged from the bathroom to find my grandma doing dishes. Despite my attempts to take over so that she could rest, she insisted, and waved me away with a flick of her dishtowel. I watched sleepily as she cleaned.

"What's that on the floor, grandma?" I pointed to a darkened spot on the brown linoleum. "Oh, that," she paused to look over her shoulder. "That's where your grandfather dropped a half-gallon of chocolate milk the other day. Spilled the whole thing. It went everywhere. I got up what I could, but he was supposed to mop the floor. He was supposed to do that yesterday, but..." She quietly went back to the dishes.

I picked up a rag and began scrubbing the remnants of mishap from the floor, the side of the oven, the bottom of the refrigerator, and their bedroom door frame. As I wiped away the dark spots, I suddenly found myself with a particularly strange thought: if I cleaned too well and removed every stain, would we have anything left of him to hold onto?

For the next several hours, I watched my grandmother flutter from room to room of their small modular home, anxious and uncertain. She shifted from countertop to drawer, exasperatingly tending to Charlie's recent attempts to put away the Tupperware or properly fold the laundry. Beneath the frustration, I could hear the longing; for him to fix things, to apologize, or just to simply...be there.

If you know Charlie at all, you know that he is Carol's fourth child who never left home. Despite his deep love for her and commitment to working hard for his family, he has always been an ornery fellow. His poorly timed practical jokes and much-too-literal interpretations of Carol's instructions sometimes left him with a lecture perfectly well-suited for an elementary school student. He never meant any harm, of course, but Carol didn't always find his antics amusing.

Now, as I watched her rearrange the cabinets, there was a different tune to her irritation. In that moment, it seemed that she would rather him be at home causing her trouble, than miss him.

.⁻.. ⁻⁻⁻ ⁻. ⁻⁻. .. ⁻. ⁻⁻.

I didn't sleep for 36 hours. My exhaustion was beginning to wilt away any remaining facade of strength. That night, my aunt drove me to the hospital so that I could visit with Charlie. I carried with me a piece of cherry pie: his favorite.

The room was a box just big enough for a bed and a single plastic chair in the corner. I held his tired and depleted hand and smiled with determination from behind my N-95 mask. Our conversation was less of an interaction than it was a recitation of stories from his years on the ball field; stories I had heard many times before, but never took for granted in hearing again. I listened as he soothed himself with his own history. He was still in there, but sometimes struggled to emerge from beneath the heavy exhaustion. I gave him a masked kiss goodbye and turned to leave, barely making it into the hallway before my walls came tumbling to the Earth.

The perplexing thing about Florida is not its high volume of elderly retirees, but rather the lack of facilities that can effectively meet their aging needs. Over the next few days, my grandpa was a perfect patient, so long as his wife was in the room. But as soon as her presence was no longer there, Charlie's mind began to wander. Despite his state of fragility and apparent weakness during our individualized visitations, his desire to be with Carol gave him an unexpected strength after sundown. We received repeated calls from nurses, complaining that he spent tireless nights escaping into the hallway and going room by room in search of his life partner and love.

Charlie was admitted to three different facilities, but none of them were able to accommodate his need for rehabilitation as well as his flighty and incoherent tendencies. In some regard, the stories were entertaining, as the staff would find him hanging clothes from the window and decorating the curtains with hospital supplies in an attempt to get the attention of someone outside, so that they might help him escape. His behaviors were strange and inexplicable, but we all knew he had one goal in mind; to be with his wife.

Back at the condo, my grandma was becoming understandably more scattered than normal. For the last several decades they had fallen into a comfortable routine. My grandpa is in charge of laundry, garbage, and miscellaneous cleaning, while my grandma cooks, manages doctor's appointments, and helps them both stay in touch with the family. They remind each other to take their medications and check their blood pressure. My grandma still advises on his daily attire, and my grandpa still sets out her nightgown on the bed at night. Without each other, they were lost.

Josh accompanied us one afternoon to visit with Charlie through the screen of a first-floor window. With more than one of us finally able to converse at once, Grandpa was coming back to full life. He was making jokes, recalling details, and throwing in a silly face every now and then. We called Chuckie on the phone to say hello, and I watched tears come to Charlie's eyes as he listened to his eldest son proudly report the results from his recent shooting competition. It felt like things were back to normal, if not for the persistence of the towering screened divider.

My grandpa has long been one of the most important people in my life, so when I began dating Josh, and I saw the way my grandpa interacted with him, I knew for certain I'd found a keeper. With every visit, my grandpa grew more attached to Josh, and it became quite clear that, in many ways, he saw his younger self in him. Josh's athleticism and gentle kindness, along with his quirky sense of humor and unwavering adoration for "his woman"—as my grandpa might say—was a modern reflection of Charlie as he was falling madly in love with Carol in the 1940s.

Before we left, Grandpa called Josh to come closer to his window. From the other side of the shaded window of the rehabilitation center, my grandpa looked at Josh with seriousness and said, "Josh, you take care of my wife for me, okay?" I smiled, thinking it sweet that he placed such an, albeit somewhat old-fashioned, task into my future husband's loving hands. He continued, "You give her a kiss from me and tell her I love her very much." It was the greatest gesture of respect and trust I had ever witnessed my grandpa place in someone I'd brought into his life. He entrusted Josh to step up and care for his family and wife in his absence. My grandpa recognized in Josh the genuine compassion that I fell in love with at that small New Year's Eve party in 2016.

I suppose I spent too many years waiting for a guy to sweep me off my feet when what I truly wanted was someone to ground me in what already was. I spent too much energy trying to convince myself and my loved ones that **this** partner was the one. When, in reality, if it was truly meant to be, they would already know. Perhaps I spent too long searching for the man that would make me whole, and not enough time for the man who would steadfastly remind me that I already am.

I knew then what my grandpa seemed to know all along; I had finally found the Charlie to my Carol.

Without a facility that could protect my grandpa during his restless nights, we had no other option but to bring him back to the condo. But with time and in-home therapy, and the now-reliable presence and support of his best friend and lifelong love, he steadily improved. Although he still gets dazed and sometimes confused, he's very much still the Charlie we all know and love. He still reminds me to never stop smiling, and always responds to an, "I love you, Grandpa," with a mischievous smile and a playful, "I know, Erin. You have to."

Carol and Charlie Yarletts are an emblem of love unparalleled to most relationships I know. And, as I lay awake in the hours before we left to return home from Florida, I realized something new:

To love someone that deeply is to also know the burden of their absence.

Whether the first few months of engagement or 67 long years spent together, a love that runs that deep also comes with the looming fear of inevitable loss. Understanding and accepting this loss, is the purest and most beautiful form of love I have ever experienced.

After years of dreaming what my future might look like, and months of meticulous planning, the day had finally arrived: October 15th, 2021. My heartbeat shook the fingers that wrapped around my bouquet, the doors standing tall before me. With a momentary pause, though void of doubt, I nodded with gratitude, and suddenly, Josh was all I could see.

67 years after my grandparents spoke their vows in that packed church in small-town Pennsylvania, I walked down the aisle and began my own legacy in love. My husband kissed me at the altar and dipped me into his right arm before we raised our hands to the sky and danced out of the ceremony space. How times have changed since September of 1954.

The Hallmark Channel wasn't introduced to the world until decades after Carol Cox and Charles Yarletts fell in love. I can't be certain what made them fall in love, or what even drew them into one another's orbit. For, when I finally found the words to ask, they simply replied, "It just was. And we just were."

The last time I visited my grandparents' home, I noticed hanging from their fridge a small piece of card stock. It read:

Do all the good you can.
By all the means you can.
In all the ways you can.
In all the places you can.
At all the times you can.
To all the people you can.
As long as ever you can.
- John Wesley

As seemingly simple an idea such as kindness and love, I thought about how drastically different the world often feels today.

I wish I could say that my pilgrimage to Amish Country provided the answers to a life filled with love and unconditionality; that the preserved structures of decades past, met with the new hair salons and trendy breweries helped me understand the complexities of living a full and vivacious life. I wish I could tell you that I discovered the trick and bottled its properties so that anyone might take advantage of its alluring possibilities.

But, the beautiful thing about kindness and a life of grace is its persistently inexplicable presence. Maybe knowing the formula would remove too many of its critical qualities. Perhaps having the answers would ruin the magic.

As I walked through the streets of Pulaski that February, where many neighbors still have yet to leave their hometown—where the Yarletts name still lingers in the air—I began to understand something profound about the way our world has transformed. We are constantly inundated with a sense of connection, driven by our smart phones and global chat rooms. But, perhaps the connective joints that keep our communities moving forward need to be a little more intentional and a lot less involuntary.

It's easy to exist on a social news feed, but it takes time and energy to bake a pie. It's courteous to bring in your trash bins at night, but truly thoughtful when you look out for your neighbors. It's common to participate in an enthusiastic day of communal volunteer work, but it takes intention to deeply care for those you serve.

In today's world, it's nearly impossible not to find connection in one way or another. But, when the connections we maintain are as passive as "liking" a status, it's no wonder we yearn for something deeper; something real. How can we expect to find sincerity in love when people are not at the center of our connections?

The small-town sense of community and lifelong sources of connection that my grandparents embraced still exist, but it's a little more difficult to find in the noise of the age of the Internet.

•••

Several months later I returned to Pennsylvania to yet again attempt to capture the essence of a beloved small town. What I found instead was a sense that I had arrived home to somewhere I never lived. I could barely get in a hand shake or share my name before hearing, "Now that's a Yarletts smile if I've ever seen one."

What is the essence of small-town America? A place where smiles are remembered for generations.

As my weekend in Pulaski came to a close and we turned onto route 18 in pursuit of the state border, my mom offered one last stop. I could feel my breath catching in my throat as my now-husband slowly lifted his foot from the accelerator and looked over at me with anticipation. We coasted another quarter-mile downhill before I cautiously admitted to myself that it was maybe now or never.

Josh turned the car around in an unsuspecting driveway and headed back to the intersection where we turned left into the Neshannock Cemetery. Thick layers of snowing ice covered the ground so that only the most prominent of headstones emerged. I squinted as the sun reflected off of every surface.

We slid carefully across the frozen top layer of our family plot. There was Buzzy, Charlie's youngest brother, who was killed in a car accident just before his 20th birthday. There were Charlie's parents, George and Mildred Yarletts. My great-grandma Mildred held me shortly after I was born, and shortly before she passed. And then, just across the driveway, Charlie and Carol's names appeared above the snow.

Protruding just above the layer of ice was the Yarletts name engraved on a polished grey marble surface. On the left was Charles L., birth year 1932, with a masonic emblem just below the R. On the right was Carol Cox, birth year 1935. In classic Yarletts comedy, we called the family to let them know the death dates had not yet been added.

After years of dreaming what their future might look like, and decades of showering the world with compassion and kindness, the day is yet to come. But when it does, they will leave behind a legacy unparalleled to any other.

Years ago, my grandparents planned and paid for their ultimate journey. Their headstone, funeral, and even their burial outfits are already accounted and paid for. A gesture that could be considered morbid, or even haunting in the face of our own mortality, hadn't made sense to me until I immersed myself in their story. For, even in their fear of losing one another, of being separated from the people around which they've built their entire life, they kept service, kindness, and compassion at the center of it all.

Love stories can be complicated, and relationships aren't always easy, but love itself doesn't have to be hard. The legacy my grandparents began back home in Pennsylvania will continue to live on in the hearts of those whose lives they have impacted with their compassion and love. They have taught us all what it means to give selflessly, support unconditionally, and cherish endlessly. Those small-town values they grew up with will live on with those who remain.

When the day comes that those dates are etched into their joint eternal resting place, they will leave behind one final gift of selflessness, to lessen the burden no matter how heavy it weighs. To allow those left behind to come together and just be, without the worry of what comes next. For even in their final journey, Carol Cox and Charles Yarletts have found a way to keep loving.

September 11, 2021
67th Wedding Anniversary

-.... --.... / -..-- . .- .-. ...

One month after this story debuted at the Northlands Storytelling Network Fringe Festival, Carol Joan Cox Yarletts finished writing her final chapter. Surrounded by loved ones and washed in prayers from all over the world, she decided that the 86 beautiful years of life she was blessed to live, was worthy of a peaceful ending.

For five days, Carol's family and friends gathered around her to share memories and show gratitude. We cried a lot, but laughed even more. Despite the sorrow and fear of a world without her, we embraced every last moment of her comedy and sass. She was at peace with her decision, and we were comforted knowing that pain and suffering would no longer be her burden to carry.

Charlie brought her a bouquet of everlasting roses. Her eldest, Chuckie, made balloon friends out of rubber gloves, and drew silly faces on them to keep her company at night. My mom, Carol Lynne, fed her ice chips and sips of tea. Her youngest, Chris, made sure that, however seating was arranged, Charlie could reach out to hold Carol's hand.

It was difficult to process what was unfolding, the reality of the decisions being made. I was terrified of what was yet to come, but somehow comforted by the space we occupied together. Charlie's sobs shook me to my very core; it was a weight even the strongest of athletes shouldn't have to carry. Although, it was one that we all knew we wouldn't have to carry alone.

We were fortunate to have so much time to say goodbye. The day she moved to hospice was nothing short of poetic. That morning, we circled her bed as Chuckie read 2 Corinthians 5-15. I played for her the song that she and grandpa danced to at our wedding, after being announced the longest married couple in the room. Chris and his wife Nean asked for a little extra love for Carol to carry with her to heaven. Outside, two rainbows appeared against a somber sky.

All afternoon we gathered joyfully around her. If not for the persistent beeping of monitors and the faint smell of a hospital, you would have thought it was just a Yarletts family reunion, which was exactly what Carol wanted it to be. Between the menu of chips, cookies, and sodas from the nurses, the decor of smiling rubber gloves, and the Solo cups filled with hard candy, it was the goodbye party we all needed.

That night, a pastor from a nearby church gave her final communion. We all cried as Psalms Chapter 23 was spoken aloud in unison. I watched as her face softened and her breathing steadied.

Upon arrival at the hospice house, Carol was making friends with the night nurses and chugging Ginger Ale. It felt odd to be there; her vitals had improved and mobility strengthened. She appeared to be recovering, and we all wondered if perhaps she might walk out on her own. Before we left, she thanked me, and whispered one more I love you.

Carol Joan Cox Yarletts was a woman of strength and conviction. She always knew what she wanted and never failed to bring it to fruition. She taught for 36 years, brought three children into the world despite all odds, and never spent a day wasted in negativity. She said she was ready, and ready she was. When we arrived the next morning, she was unresponsive, tired from the days of celebration.

Charlie sat in the recliner next to her bed, holding her hand and napping in the afternoons. By the time her final visitors arrived to say goodbye, Carol's breathing was more labored. The gentle snoring that masked an impending absence, now became a clearer sound of transition. She had fought to be with us all until the very end, but with goodbyes said and gratitudes whispered, it was time to rest.

We all took turns speaking the words we wished we had earlier and then some. Carol Lynne did her hair for the last time. I ran my fingers alongside my grandma's face and finally allowed myself to cry over her as I thanked her for her influence in my life. My uncle played Ave Maria for her one last time. Charlie laid his hand gently across her cheek and forehead. We all held each other in bittersweet sadness.

Before we left, Charlie leaned over his wife of 67 years, his best friend of many more, and said, "One more for the road, woman." As his lips neared hers for the very last time, an indescribable force of love overtook the room, when–despite two days of immobility–Carol turned her head to meet him.

Later that night, as her family spent the evening grilling burgers and playing with sparklers, I like to imagine that she might have smiled, proud to leave behind a legacy of joy. She knew that we would care for each other in her absence, and that we would honor her well-lived life by continuing to create something beautiful of our own.

Carol Joan Cox Yarletts left this Earth
on Memorial Day, 2022,
but we will never truly be without her.

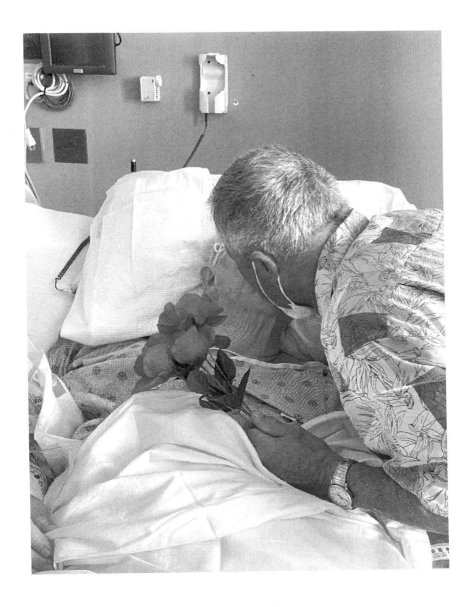

Made in the USA
Middletown, DE
06 November 2023